Little Wonder

A song, book, and memory keeper

Created by:

The Saturn
Creative Team

A traveling homeschool family

Illustrated by: Kata Upama

www.saturnmusicandentertainment.com

This book belongs to

Insert baby image here

_____

Welcome, Little Wonder,
to the playground we call Earth.

You have a secret garden
with miles of hillside and mountain peaks.

Rivers, lakes, streams, ocean waves;
the sky colored in blue.

Sparkles on the waters edge
are dancing just for you.

Wander, Little Wonder,
on the playground we call Earth.

Look up to greet the sunshine
and feel its warm rays reach out to you.

Treetops, ferns, soft mossy rocks,
and canopies of green.

Forest glades are natures way
to keep your playground clean.

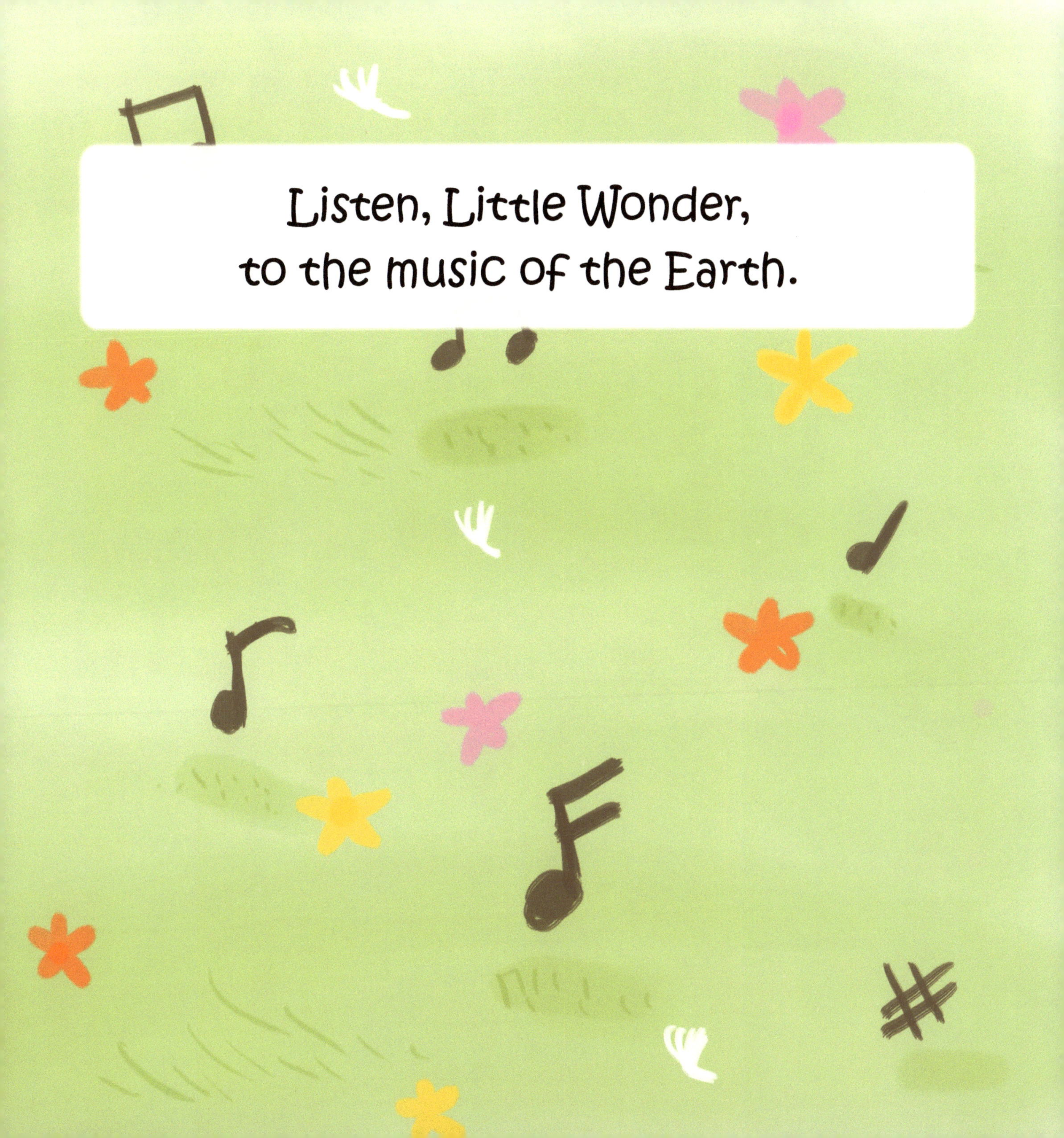

Listen, Little Wonder,
to the music of the Earth.

It plays as the wind blows;
a special song made just for you.

Rustling leaves, the ocean breeze,
sing harmonies in tune.

Can you hear the symphonies
playing just for you?

Welcome, Little Wonder,
to the playground we call Earth.

Little Wonder

Music by: The Saturn Creative Team

To download the Little Wonder music,
go to www.saturnmusicandentertainment.com/music

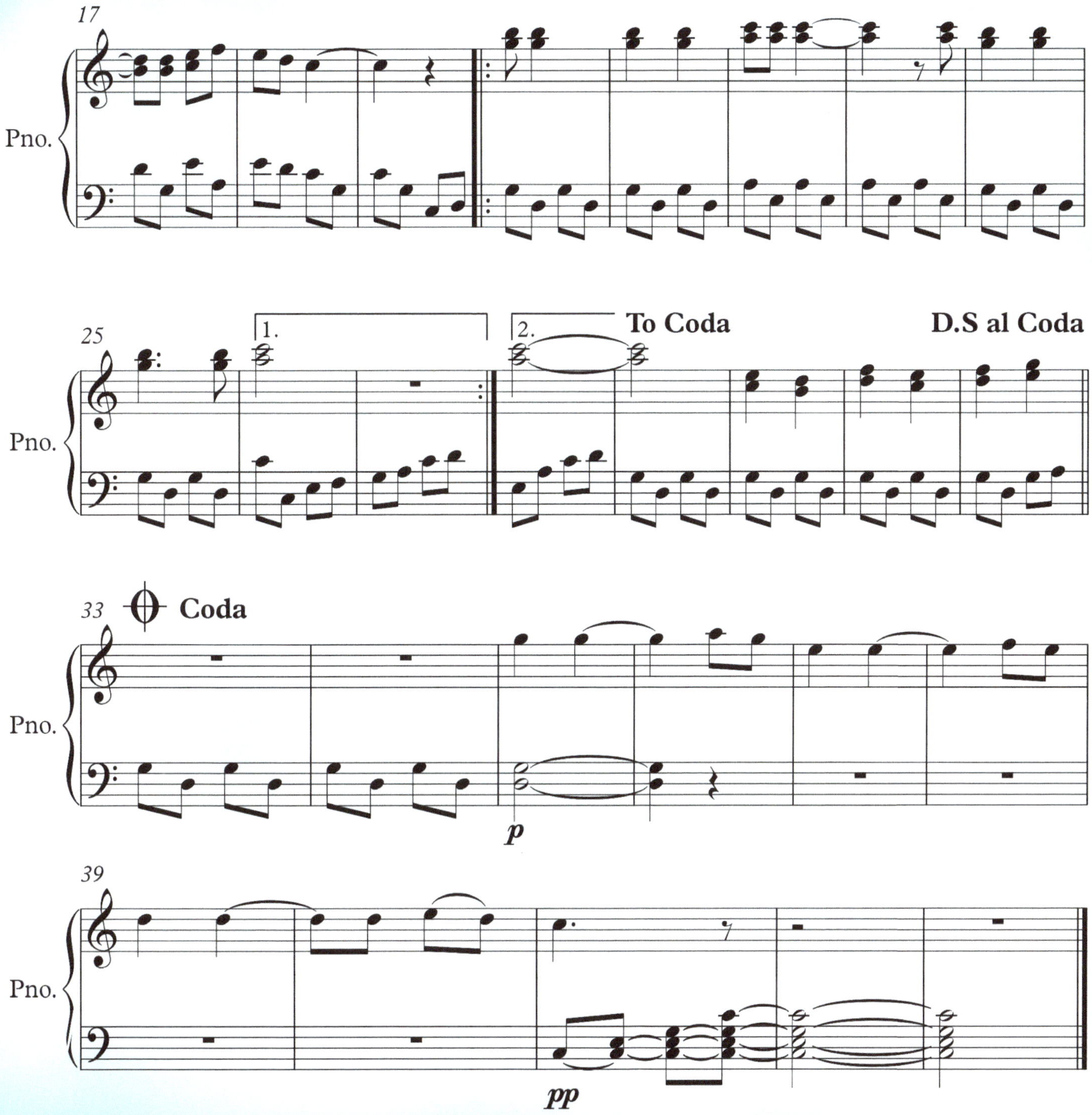
17
Pno.
25
1.
2.
To Coda
D.S al Coda
33
Coda
p
39
pp

When I Was Born

The President was

I lived in

A cup of coffee cost

Going to the movies cost

The weather was

It was popular to

The news headline was

The family car was

The #1 hit song was

The #1 novel was

My Hands

_____

Date

My Feet

_____
Date

Milestones

First smile	First laugh

First word	First crawled

First steps

First tooth

First bath

First vacation

First food

First hug

example:
Happiness
starts within

Words of Wisdom

Wishes for Baby

I hope you love: _____

I hope you laugh: _____

I hope you remember: _____

I hope you have: _____

I hope you learn: _____

I hope you always: _____

Love,

_____

My First Year

Month 1:

Month 2:

Month 3:

Month 4:

Month 5:

Month 6:

Month 7:

Month 8:

Month 9:

Month 10:

Month 11:

Month 12:

Insert birthday image here

My Hands

Month 12

_____
Date

About The Authors

the BOSS

the HEART & SOUL

The Brains

Meet The Saturn Creative Team, a traveling homeschool family with creative spirit.

Together, this family creates and produces entertainment for kids such as books, music, activities and more.

Connect with The Saturn Creative Team and follow their adventures as they travel the world and continue their education journey.

Learn more about the team at:
www.saturnmusicandentertainment.com

www.ingramcontent.com/pod-product-compliance
Lightning Source LLC
LaVergne TN
LVHW072053070426
835508LV00002B/81